PRE-RAPHAELITES AT THE OFFICE

Carol McKendrick

NEW HOLLAND

Introduction

We all know the paintings of the Pre-Raphaelites – beautiful women trapped in medieval chambers. After years of research, financed by demeaning temporary work, I am now in a position to singlehandedly overthrow this pre-conception. Far from being the idealized dream-world fit only for calendars and address books, the world the Pre-Raphaelites wanted to inhabit was as real and as shocking as any unmade bed you'd care to imagine.

The Pre-Raphaelites produced a parallel output of work they termed their 'Office' art. This has all the usual features of Pre-Raphaelite paintings but instead of the heroine being in her customary malaise, she is shown sitting at a computer or waiting for the microwave to ping. At a brushstroke these apathetic women become working girls.

After the office had been invented by Charles Dickens, it became ever more a feature of Victorian life. The Pre-Raphaelites' endless depictions of computerized drudgery, though, were not to the taste of the artists' patrons – the very businessmen who had founded the companies employing these Silicone Sallies or PC Prossies, two of the more acceptable sobriquets for the new, predominantly female workforce. Added to this, when the Pre-Raphaelites exhibited their unsentimental Office paintings, showing what real life was like for Victorian working girls, they caused outrage among critics and public alike.

The Pre-Raphaelites knew which side their bread was buttered and the Office art was shoved to the back of the studio and given to family and friends for Christmas, only to percolate further and further away from the eyes of the art establishment. Until now...

I have unearthed nearly 80 examples of the Pre-Raphaelites' Office work, although when my current manager caught me writing this on my computer in work time and gave me my first warning, she said I was wasting everyone's time. What does she know? She thinks she knows all about art because she once found herself in the Tate Britain shop while looking for a public toilet.

Pre-Raphaelism began in autumn 1848, when a group of young Cockney art students began calling themselves the Pre-Raphaelite Boys. They kept their names top secret and signed their work 'PRB'. The Boys began painting in a simple vivid medieval style, which historically came before the style of Raphael – a top Renaissance artist. The formation of the Pre-Raphaelite Boys is generally credited to 20-year-old Gabriel Charles Dante Rossetti (1828–82), who, with a little bit of tweaking, gave himself one of the best names in painting. Dante Gabriel Rossetti was born in London where his father was a Victorian asylum seeker. He became an art student at the Royal Academy where he met the second member of the group, William Holman Hunt (1827–1910), nicknamed 'The Maniac'. Hunt's best friend, John Everett 'Bubbles' Millais (1829–96), became the third member and Rossetti enrolled his brother, his sister's boyfriend and two people who couldn't paint. The rest is art history.

The aim of the secret seven was to revolutionize current styles of painting, which the Boys thought were 'slosh' – the fussy style of Sir 'Sloshua' Reynolds – and 'filth' – Rubens' nudie ladies. They wanted to paint things from nature as they really were, or 'up close and personal', as Rossetti put it. No amount of detail was too much and one couldn't be too careful: indeed it took Holman Hunt three weeks to paint the letters 'PRB'. Everything was painted in day-glo colours, but perhaps most startling was the decision by the Pre-Raphaelites to set their super-modern Victorian pictures in the Middle Ages. The Boys felt that the olden days were simpler, purer times than the self-interested rampant capitalism and materialism of their own era, and as Millais said, 'Nostalgia sells.'

Pre-Raphaelism was also a poetic movement, strongly influenced by the work of Keats and Tennyson, who stole medieval storylines. Rossetti and his sister churned out vague and morbid poetry respectively.

It was Rossetti who completed the first Pre-Raphaelite Office picture in 1849 with *IT Training – Trouble with the Mouse* (Plate 12) which he signed 'PRO', an acronym for 'Pre-Raphaelites at the Office'. It is a depiction of the Virgin Mary, but Raphael's standard virgin this ain't. No clouds or cherubs surround her, only the impedimenta of

Above: IT Training – Trouble With The Mouse, *Dante Gabriel Rossetti, 1849 (Plate 12)*

the office girl: rucksack, mobile and bottled water. The young Virgin Mary is sitting at her computer being given Information Technology training by some old boot. The usual stunning Renaissance blue of Mary's robe is here reserved for the Virgin's mousemat. The computer is painted in photographic detail but the training takes place in a medieval room and it is this juxtaposition of the medieval and modern that heightens our response. We think, '*Did they have computers in medieval times?*' The picture says it all about office work: boredom through the ages.

Rossetti used his sister Christina as the model for Mary in the picture, and she features again as the hunched office girl on the back foot in *Manager in Uncomfortable Shoes* (Plate 38). At the time of painting, in 1850, call-centres had just been introduced and Christina wears the now familiar call-centre head-dress. The manager is just like the manager of today, wandering round the office doing nothing and picking on people… Speak of the devil, here comes mine.

The Pre-Raphaelites were always on the lookout for 'stunners' to model for their paintings, in the hope that one thing would lead to another, and for Rossetti – on the small side but with the Vesuvian good looks of his Italian heritage – it usually did.

Above Top: Going To Be Late, *John Everett Millais, 1852 (Plate 1)*

Above: The Boss's Office, *William Holman Hunt, 1853 (Detail, Plate 20)*

It was Millais who first had the archetypal Pre-Raphaelite stunner Lizzie Siddall (1829–62) sit for him in an office painting – or rather lie. Spotted working in a branch of 'Top Bonnet' off Leicester Square, Lizzie had a neck like a giraffe's and a mass of red hair. Millais had her pose as Hamlet's zany girlfriend Ophelia, Shakespeare being another favourite Pre-Raphaelite author. In *Going To Be Late* (Plate 1), Lizzie posed in a shrink-to-fit ball gown, lying in Millais' parents' luxury jacuzzi jet system bath, the surface of the water strewn with potpourri – all pointing to the fact that Ophelia was not up for another day at the office.

When Rossetti met Lizzie he knocked out the second 'L' of her surname, told her that only he was allowed to paint her, and she was enslaved.

This left models like Annie Miller for Holman Hunt. The Bill Wyman of the group, Hunt wrote a two-volume history of the Pre-Raphaelites, claiming he had thought of everything from Pre-Raphaelism to William Morris' Arts and Crafts Movement. Hunt writes that he and Morris went into a branch of 'Sofa Workhouse', where Morris had a panic attack due the shoddiness of the furniture. Hunt claims he gave Morris the idea of revolutionizing the soft furnishings' trade when trying to calm him down.

With his intense X-ray eyes undressing everything he saw and filling in details where others feared to look, there is no denying Hunt was off-putting. But, with a promise of an introduction to Rossetti, he managed to get his share of girlfriends, of which Annie Miller was one.

Not all the Office paintings are in medieval settings and Hunt's *The Boss's Office* (Plate 20) is set in modern-day Victorian London. Annie Miller poses as a secretary: she has just got up from sitting on her boss's knee having noticed something out of the window. Hunt paints what she has seen for the viewer in the mirror at the rear of the office: just visible on the left is the then newly-built Post Office Tower.

Something else the Pre-Raphaelites are famous for is symbolism. In their mainstream pictures this takes the form of long-forgotten medieval Christian symbolism, which meant nothing to anyone even by Victorian times, so in fact was just irritating. In their Office art, the symbolism is bang on. Who can fail to spot the boss's intentions with the phallic symbol of the Post Office Tower looming in the background? There is further symbolism in what the art critic John Ruskin (1819–1900) called the 'fatal newness' of the furniture: the red light, the black leather chair, the executive fish tank, all shriek, 'Creep!'

Although call-centres were taking off in Victorian times, prostitution was still the number one occupation for girls with no qualifications. The Pre-Raphaelites were very interested in prostitutes because, as well as painting in a medieval way, they adopted a medieval code of chivalry and felt that mixing with prostitutes and working class girls was the gentlemanly thing to do. Hunt's concern for fallen women was such that he proposed to Annie Miller, who, if she hadn't exactly fallen, was certainly wobbly.

By 1853 the Pre-Raphaelites' mainstream work was popular with buyers and the public. This was in no small part due to the praise and patronage of the aforementioned critic, John Ruskin. Ruskin had declared Millais' *The Photocopier Room* (Plate 53) to be the best depiction of lower-back pain in art history – thus vindicating Millais' decision to use only models with repetitive strain injuries. That summer, Ruskin and his wife Effie were holidaying in Scotland, and Millais was invited to accompany them and paint the critic's portrait. Although he would have preferred to have gone Inter-railing with the rest of the Boys on the new Victorian railways, Millais' latent commercialism forced him to the Trossachs.

The Ruskins had been married five years but their marriage remained unconsummated due to Ruskin discovering that his bride was not like the classical statues he knew so intimately, but had pubic hair. On holiday Millais gave Effie drawing lessons and the two became close. When she returned to London, Effie spoke to a girlfriend whose father was an obstetrician and who made it clear to Effie what her marriage was missing. Effie spoke to Millais, Millais spoke to Effie's parents and then someone spoke to a newspaper. The Ruskins' ensuing divorce scandal knocked even the Crimean War off the front pages.

Despite everything, Millais honourably finished the portrait, but Ruskin was not pleased with the result. Consciously or unconsciously, Millais went into Office art mode and gave Ruskin a bottle of Evian, a carrier bag and red varnished fingernails (Plate 19).

In 1854 Holman Hunt decided to go to Israel and paint it in lurid colours. In 1855 Millais married Effie, the now ex-wife of John 'Psycho-sexual Problems' Ruskin, and went into advertising. Christina Rossetti broke up with her boyfriend and Rossetti was forever engaged in rows and reconciliations with his long-time girlfriend Lizzie Siddal. It looked like the Pre-Raphaelite Boys were all washed up, or were they?

Two young men up at Oxford University had all the Pre-Raphaelite credentials. Young, male, alienated and out of touch, William Morris (1834–96) and Edward Burne-Jones (1833–98) were a couple of Camelot freaks who longed for a time machine to take them back to the Middle Ages. Dante Gabriel Rossetti was to be their very own Doctor Who.

Burne-Jones was a Brummie born plain Edward Jones but, taking his cue from Hunt's flop of an invented double-barrelled name, firmly shackled himself with a hyphen. His mother died a few days after his birth and he was a delicate and sickly child. Being stabbed at school in morning assembly didn't help and Burne-Jones remained wimpish for the rest of his life.

William Morris was the absolute opposite of his etiolated friend. Tubby, vital and loaded, the one thing Morris had in common with Burne-Jones was a love of the olden days. Having been given a made-to-measure suit of armour as a boy, Morris' medieval daydreams started early. In 1857 Rossetti was employed by the university to give the Student Union a double coat of the Middle Ages. Like Burne-Jones, Morris was only too delighted to help out.

Although Rossetti was now pushing 30, he was still chasing stunners all over Oxford. Ostensibly to use as a model for the medieval murals they were painting, he found 17-year-old Janey Burden (1839–1914). Tall and brooding with a lot of hair, Janey's father was a groom and she had a thick yokel accent. But as long as she kept her mouth shut no one cared. She was to become the Pre-Raphaelite supermodel.

William Morris painted Janey in 1858 in *Getting Dressed* (Plate 4). A girl stands in her bedroom getting ready to go to work. In the foreground, the girl's all-important volumizer hairdryer stands in a brass jug, its black spikes hammering out of the painting like a medieval torture instrument. Once again the Pre-Raphaelite Office symbolism hits home. This was to be Morris' only oil painting due to his departure into the Victorian interior design market, but it clearly expresses the feelings of pointlessness that are the backbone of the office girl's existence. The all-pervasive sadness of the picture is overwhelming, despite Medieval Radio One being on in the background of the painting in the form of a man singing and playing.

Janey's look of self-absorbed hopelessness was perhaps caused by the fact that, although it was the dangerously fanciable Rossetti who discovered her, it was the over-stuffed chintzy Morris who proposed. With a background like hers this was a proposal in a million and Janey and Morris married in 1859, with none of his horrified family present. Morris left the painting unfinished and presciently it was to be Rossetti who finished Janey off.

Burne-Jones was about to marry Georgie Macdonald, who wasn't a stunner so appeared in none of his Office paintings, and Rossetti began to feel he ought to do the decent thing. He married Lizzie Siddal in 1860 and a double honeymoon was planned with the Burne-Joneses, but they didn't turn up due to Burne-Jones collapsing with nervous exhaustion on the way to Dover. Georgie had to sedate him with turps.

A trio of happy marriages this was not to be, more a Victorian *Posy of Barbed Wire*. But the more tangled and tortuous things became, the more the artists turned to their Office paintings for consolation.

For Lizzie the honeymoon was over a long time ago. By 1862 she was a confirmed melancholic and, in a true famous-person-style death, took a suicidal drug overdose. Rossetti was devastated. It was said that he was with a lady-friend on the night of Lizzie's death. Exactly why Rossetti flung his unpublished manuscript of poems into Lizzie's coffin to be buried with her remains unknown – if she hadn't already read them, it was too late now.

Burne-Jones, meanwhile, had found himself a stunner-and-a-half in Mary Zambaco, wife of a renowned Constantinople venereal disease expert. A wild Greek goddess with flaming red hair and lucid skin, she knew what she

was about when Burne-Jones was commissioned to paint her portrait in 1866. She became by turns his favourite model, muse and mistress. In *Morning Weigh-In* (Plate 2) Mary is daringly painted coming out of the shower. At about the time of this painting Burne-Jones tried to break with her, and Morris planned to get his friend away from Zambaco's clutches with a holiday to Rome, but once again Burne-Jones collapsed at Dover. In January 1869, Mary threatened to drown herself in Regent's Canal in front of the dithering Burne-Jones and pulled out a phial of laudanum. Burne-Jones wrestled her to the ground in full view of the public and the police were called.

In *Jogging* (Plate 67), Burne-Jones captures all the degradation of the event. He paints himself as defenceless, and originally naked, being pounced on by Mary with her phial of laudanum tucked into her jogging suit. The full-frontal male nudity of the piece outraged the Christo-wrapped Victorians and it was G. F. Watts (1817–1904), an expert in painting nudie subjects tastefully – see *The Gym,* (Plate 68), who persuaded Burne-Jones to paint on the shorts.

Burne-Jones' obsession with Mary and her presence in his paintings continued, but by *Office Lech* (Plate 52) the affair was over and Burne-Jones opted for his wife Georgie. He hadn't got the constitution for stunners and neither, as it turned out, had his friend Rossetti.

Left: The Temp: Twenty-To-Three, *Dante Gabriel Rossetti, 1868–80 (Plate 44)*

Rossetti was now living a stone's throw from Mick Jagger in Cheyne Walk with former prostitute Fanny Cornforth, part stunner, part housekeeper. Also in residence were a wombat, a kangaroo, an armadillo and depraved poet and raver Algernon Swinburne – an old friend of Lizzie's who, out of loyalty to her memory, always called Fanny 'The Bitch'. Disorder ruled and, now she was dead, Rossetti was obsessed with Lizzie and painting her beyond the grave – see *Thank God It's Friday* (Plate 60).

In 1868 Janey Morris agreed to model for him, and Rossetti began his *Temp Series*. Still under 30, Janey had lost none of her looks, although perhaps because of her accent her conversation had not developed. The playwright George Bernard Shaw described her as the most silent woman he had ever met, and it was specifically so Janey could communicate that Morris invented the wallpaper-patterned notelet.

In the first picture of the series, *The Temp: Twenty-To-Three* (Plate 44), the temp is sitting at her desk, waiting for a text message – another method of communication suitable for Janey. But it is the temp's cheap canvas handbag that dominates the picture. What a slap in the eye it must have been for Morris who could have supplied any number of yards of tasteful fabric. The handbag said it all: Janey and Rossetti were an item.

The depiction of the stunner reached its apotheosis with Rossetti's Office pictures of Janey. A further reason Office paintings triumph over their mainstream Pre-Raphaelite counterparts is because there is no pretence of the model being a medieval or mythological character to get in the way – in the *Temp Series*, it's just plain Jane Morris.

A competitive edge had always existed between Rossetti and Morris, and now that Janey was involved it sharpened

William 'Wallpaper' Morris had been having his poetry published for years and it was rubbish; Rossetti wanted his poetry published too. There was just one problem, it was six feet under with Lizzie.

As anyone who has exhumed a spouse knows, it's not an easy decision. But in the dead of a blustery autumn night in 1869, in high Gothic fashion, Rossetti's dealer and all-round fixer, Charles Howell, unearthed Lizzie from Highgate Cemetery. Rossetti was not present – only Howell, the gravediggers and a doctor standing by with a bottle of Dettol to disinfect the poems. They dug down to Lizzie's coffin and looked inside. Lizzie's body was perfectly intact and her red hair still blazing! The manuscript had not fared so well – it was soaking wet with a wormhole right through the middle.

The truth about the unearthing slowly oozed out. Swinburne said that it was with 'grave delight' he heard the poems had been retrieved. When your friends are saying things like this, you can imagine what everyone else is saying. The awful smell of the manuscript – a mix of decay and Dettol – was overcome and it was transcribed around the wormholes. Published in 1870, the poems had a haunting power, but not of the sort talked about by reviewers, and a respectable 'Penguin Book of Exhumed Poetry' they could never become.

The love affair continued and in 1871, Rossetti, Morris and Janey went to live in a three-up, three-down ménage-à-trois midway between Oxford and Swindon. Morris, unable to stand the strain, went on a prolonged holiday to Iceland. All seemed to be going well for Rossetti but that same year a bad review came out attacking his poems. It was too much. Like so many Pre-Raphaelite hangers-on Rossetti bought a phial of laudanum and drank it.

Meanwhile, Holman Hunt was *Home Again* (Plate 66) painting his hymn to the microwave. Annie Miller having married someone else, Hunt excelled himself and married two sisters, although not at the same time.

A Pre-Raphaelite Office artist who didn't fare so well was Simeon Solomon (1840–1905). Arrested for homosexual offences, he became a social leper, which is reflected in his painting *Below Stairs* (Plate 51). Solomon clearly identifies with the cleaner in the picture – a species still looked down upon by so many office workers, even though the cleaner is quite possibly earning more per hour.

A modern twist is given to landscapes in Pre-Raphaelite Office art. Inchbold's *Imagining the Weekend* (Plate 28) depicts an idyllic spring car-rally. Exhibited at the Royal Academy, the picture caused uproar when a hawk-eyed Victorian spotted two pairs of boots outside the tent and by association impropriety within. When Inchbold (1830–88) refused to paint gauze drapery over the boots the picture was hung in the Academy Tea Room and pelted with cream buns.

Thirty-six hours passed and Rossetti came round. He was a changed man. Depressed, druggy and alcoholic, Rossetti continued to paint Janey, but the affair was over. The last painting of the *Temp Series* was completed in 1880. *The Temp's Nightmare* (Plate 77) features the temp hiding up a tree, but she cannot escape from being surrounded by telephones. The nightmare has a deeper interpretation. In this picture the series' central motif of the mobile phone is missing. Rossetti called the mobile 'the Devil's toy'; it was this invention that had sanctioned his and Janey's relationship, enabling them to communicate without Morris (who was always home embroidering) picking up. In the picture, although Janey is surrounded by phones, she has no mobile: Rossetti and Janey's relationship is up a gum tree.

Although Lizzie, Janey and Mary were such a success in the Office paintings, in reality, the sexist mainstream Pre-Raphaelite image of the *femme fatale* had come home to roost. Stunners were nothing but trouble. Rossetti was a ruined man. Morris buried himself in politics under the Socialist Sofa banner. After the Zambaco fiasco, Burne-Jones was so nervous of his wife finding him out that he made all his models look the same – see *The Tube* (Plate 6). This was to prove a winning formula for the last great exponent of Pre-Raphaelite Office painting, John William Waterhouse (1849–1917).

Very little is known of Waterhouse's life; it seems his wife burnt all his papers, perhaps knowing his private life could never keep up with the Joneses and Rossettis of the movement. Or it could have been even worse. Waterhouse's use of neo-Pagan settings and wild-looking women within circles – *Corporate Barbecue* (Plate 70) and *Work Drink* (Plate 72) – has led to charges that he participated in ceremonial magic, but I will leave this to be delved into by other scholars who don't have two jobs to do at once.

Always pictured in a business suit himself, painting office girls was Waterhouse's first love. After 1890 men only appear in his Office paintings as victims, such as the hapless messenger in *Slut* (Plate 58). Indeed it is with Waterhouse that office girls lose their vacant computer gaze and become active. In *Corporate Barbecue* and *Work Drink*, the protagonists are doing things that men usually do, such as lighting the barbecue and getting drunk. But the worker bound by her own computer wires in *Teatime Tangle* (Plate 50) signifies the downside of women being tied to the office. Nor is *Breaking The Glass Ceiling* (Plate 21) the triumphant picture one would expect. A female boss with a hangover hairstyle from her phone head-set days stands pensively in her new office. As she stares into her crystal ball of a paperweight, is she already foreseeing the de-skilling of mothers and future generations of obese latchkey glue sniffers?

Corporate Fraud (Plate 36) illustrates the seamy side of office life: a woman is depicted stealing sensitive information. I would hardly say stealing stationery was in the same league, but the trouble I'm in, you'd think so

Waterhouse perceived the trend towards corporate hospitality. The infiltration of the unwanted businessman is soundly dealt with in *Henley – The Search For The Corporate Guest* (Plate 55). The weather is gloomy and there is no sign of the guest on the river, except perhaps for the half submerged bottle of *Moet & Chandon*. Although not as overtly as Fredrick Sandys (1829–1904) in *You Don't Have To Be Mad To Work Here…* (Plate 56) and *Twenty-to-Five Panic* (Plate 59), Waterhouse painted working women with mental health problems: the female cyclist in *Eco-Warrior* (Plate ?) is clearly deranged. In this same painting Waterhouse takes a side-swipe at the Victorian love of branded goods: the girl can't afford a decent bike but she has a Louis Vuitton handbag.

Like Burne-Jones, Waterhouse was criticised for painting the same face over and over again. In Waterhouse's case this was unfair, as many of his models were in fact identical, having been provided by the recently-opened London model agency 'Capital Nymph'.

Rossetti died in 1882. Burne-Jones didn't make the funeral, breaking down at the station as usual. Millais and Morris died in 1896, the sickly Burne-Jones lasting two years longer. Hunt died in 1910 leaving only Waterhouse to keep the faith, despite the fact that Pre-Raphaelism was becoming less and less fashionable. In 1917 the announcement of Waterhouse's death in *The Times* was buried among lists of lost soldiers. Pre-Raphaelism was dead and the Office art already forgotten.

So my story is at an end, not only because I've been sacked from my job for personal use of work-time and stationery – obviously the global unearthing of national art treasures is unimportant when compared to temping for an insurance company – but also because our odyssey has come full circle.

No wonder the women in these paintings are miserable, forever locked in the towers of their offices doing mindless work fit only for insurance clerks. Looking at these pictures makes you want to punch the clock for the last time and break free, and this is the function of true art, to give us an uncompromising inspirational experience of life. Forget farmyard animals in formaldehyde, this is the BritArt we've been waiting for!

C.M.

1. Going To Be Late

2. MORNING WEIGH-IN

3. Is That A Spot?

4. GETTING DRESSED

5. GOODBYE

6. THE TUBE

7. Eco-Warrior

8. FLOWERS FOR RECEPTION

9. THE TEMP: TEN-PAST-NINE

Rossetti recklessly displays his illicit love affair with
Mrs William Morris via his painted text message.

10. LEVER ARCH

11. New Water Cooler

12. IT Training – Trouble With The Mouse

13. Peckish

14. THE INTERVIEW

15. Knight In Reception

16. THE FILING ROOM

17. THE TEMP: TWENTY-TO-ELEVEN

18. UNLOOKED-FOR ADMIRER

19. Day Course In Executive Leadership

20. THE BOSS'S OFFICE

21. Breaking The Glass Ceiling

22. SMOKERS

23. Run Out Of Cups

24. Office Cad

25. PETTY CASH

26. Paper Jam

27. NEARLY LUNCHTIME

28. Imagining The Weekend

29. LUNCH HOUR – STAYING IN THE OFFICE

30. Alfresco

31. Hayfever

32. QUICK DIP

33. Shopping

34. Office Christmas Lunch

35. THE UNSUITABLE POST ROOM BOYFRIEND

36. CORPORATE FRAUD

37. GOING HOME SICK

38. Manager In Uncomfortable Shoes

Rossetti's wittily painted Post-Its capture the early Pre-Raphaelite movement in microcosm.

39. Meeting

40. HIGHLIGHTING HER POINT

41. PRESENTATION

42. POST-LUNCH DIP

43. THE BOARDROOM: WIMBLEDON FORTNIGHT

44. THE TEMP: TWENTY-TO-THREE

45. Mr Gorgeous In Reception

46. CAR PARK

47. LACKING MOTIVATION

48. Computer Man To The Rescue

49. Afternoon Daydream

50. Teatime Tangle

51. BELOW STAIRS

52. OFFICE LECH

53. The Photocopier Room

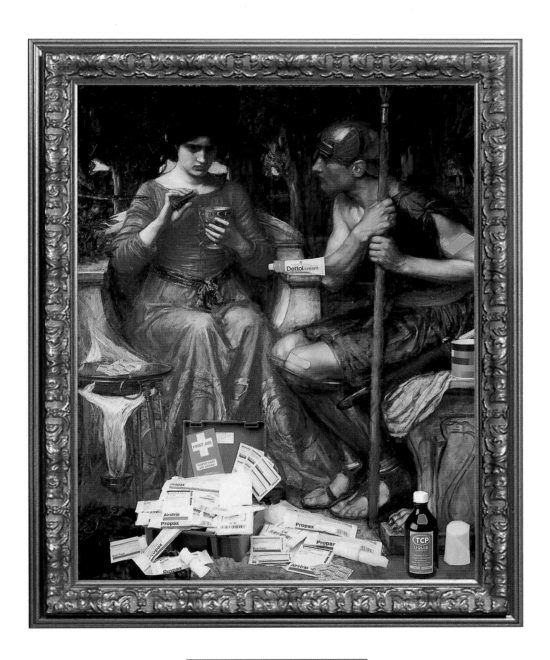

54. First-Aider

55. HENLEY – THE SEARCH FOR THE CORPORATE GUEST

56. YOU DON'T HAVE TO BE MAD TO WORK HERE...

57. THE COURIER

58. Slut

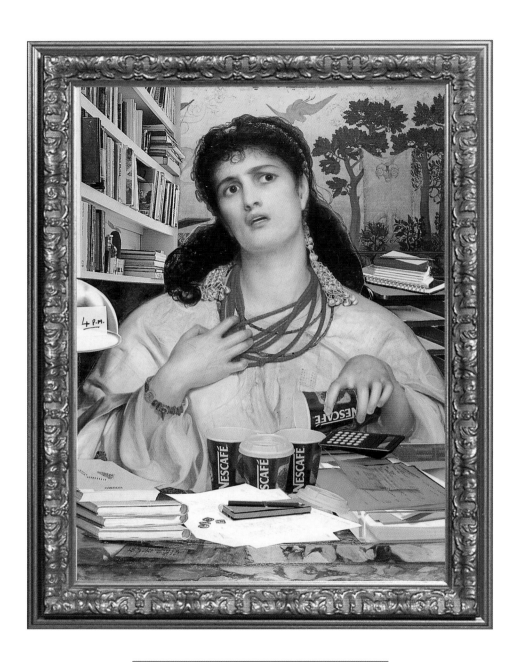

59. Twenty-To-Five Panic

60. THANK GOD IT'S FRIDAY

61. The Ladies

62. OFFICE TO EVENING TRANSFORMATION

63. BUS STOP

64. Overcrowded Public Transport

65. Praying For A Train

66. HOME AGAIN

67. JOGGING

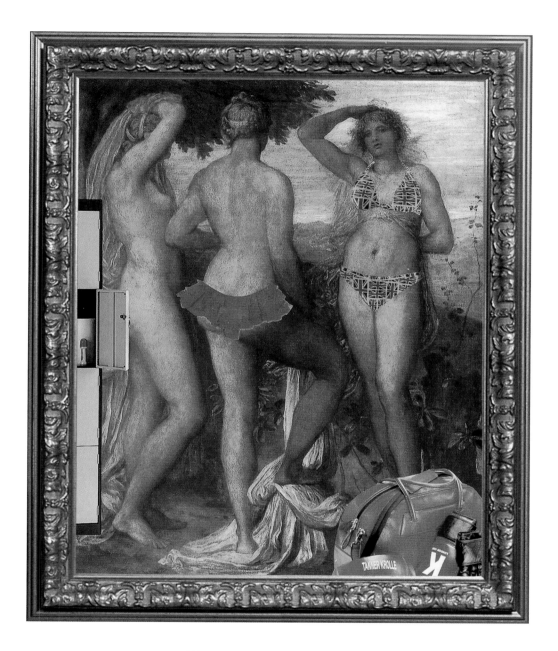

68. THE GYM

69. OFFICE CHRISTMAS PARTY

70. CORPORATE BARBECUE

71. GIRLS' NIGHT OUT

72. WORK DRINK

73. Transformation Complete

74. LAUNDRETTE

75. LATE NIGHT VISITOR

76. PRAYERS

77. THE TEMP'S NIGHTMARE

78. SWEET DREAMS

Plates

I have ordered the plates in accordance with the working day, which I think is of particular service to the paintings. C.M.

1. GOING TO BE LATE
John Everett Millais, 1852
Collection of Ronnie Wood

2. MORNING WEIGH-IN
Edward Burne-Jones, 1869
Museo de Arte Basemente, Puerto Rico

3. IS THAT A SPOT?
John William Waterhouse, 1897
Clearasil Corp., Pittsburgh

4. GETTING DRESSED
William Morris, 1858
Saga Saga Coffee Shop, Reykjavik

5. GOODBYE
William John Hennessy, 1870
Fame School, Liverpool
(Gift of Ms Jane Stothard)

6. THE TUBE
Edward Burne-Jones, 1880
Ticket Office, Finsbury Park Tube Station

7. ECO-WARRIOR
John William Waterhouse, 1910
Collection of Anita Roddick

8. FLOWERS FOR RECEPTION
John William Waterhouse, 1908
Coca Cola Institute of Product Placement, Michigan

9. THE TEMP: TEN-PAST-NINE
Dante Gabriel Rossetti, 1877
Office Angels, Bromley
(& detail)

10. LEVER ARCH
Dante Gabriel Rossetti, 1874
Alice Springs Institute of Aboriginal Art and a Few Other Things

11. NEW WATER COOLER
John William Waterhouse, 1892
Le Musee d'Art Très Moderne, Brussels

12. IT TRAINING – TROUBLE WITH THE MOUSE
Dante Gabriel Rossetti, 1849
Palazzo del Vaticano (roped-off Pope Only Area), Vatican City

13. PECKISH
John Everett Millais, 1851
Weight Watchers, Chagford

14. THE INTERVIEW
John William Waterhouse, 1887
Barber Institute, mop and bucket room, Birmingham

15. KNIGHT IN RECEPTION
Edward Burne-Jones, 1884
Rotters' Nightclub, Preston

16. THE FILING ROOM
Edward Burne-Jones, 1871
Hermitage Museum filing room, St. Petersburg

17. THE TEMP: TWENTY-TO-ELEVEN
Dante Gabriel Rossetti, 1879
Collection of Nicky Clarke

18. UNLOOKED-FOR ADMIRER
John William Waterhouse, 1912
Strangeways Prison, Manchester

19. DAY COURSE IN EXECUTIVE LEADERSHIP
John Everett Millais, 1854
(*Formerly Portrait of John Ruskin*)
Falkland Fine Art, Port Stanley

20. THE BOSS'S OFFICE
William Holman Hunt, 1853
Collection of Mr C & Mrs A Childs

21. BREAKING THE GLASS CEILING
John William Waterhouse, 1902
Collection of Baroness Thatcher

70. CORPORATE BARBECUE
John William Waterhouse, 1886
Linda McCartney Foods,
Hayes

71. GIRLS' NIGHT OUT
Dante Gabriel Rossetti, 1872
Terracotta Gallery, Beijing

72. WORK DRINK
John William Waterhouse, 1891
Musée des Beaux Arts,
Basingstoke

73. TRANSFORMATION
COMPLETE
Dante Gabriel Rossetti, 1866
Two's Company Unisex Hairdressers,
Wolverhampton

74. LAUNDRETTE
John William Waterhouse, date unknown
Spin Me Round Laundrette, Liverpool

75. LATE NIGHT VISITOR
Edward Burne-Jones, 1896
Reader's Digest Art Collection, Delaware

76. PRAYERS
Edward Burne-Jones, 1863
Heathrow Airport Multi-Faith
Prayer Room – Terminal Two

77. THE TEMP'S
NIGHTMARE
Dante Gabriel Rossetti, 1880
Faroe Islands Hospital Secure Unit

78. SWEET DREAMS
Edward Burne-Jones, 1870
Kind permission of Mr John Bedford

SELECT BIBLIOGRAPHY

Anne Clark Amor, *William Holman Hunt, The True Pre-Raphaelite*, 1989

Percy H. Bate, *The English Pre-Raphaelite Painters*, 1899

Helen Dore, *William Morris*, 1990

Penelope Fitzgerald, *Edward Burne-Jones*, 1975

William Holman Hunt, *Pre-Raphaelitism and the Pre-Raphaelite Brotherhood*, 1905

Charles Augustus Howell, *Rossetti Spaghetti – Rossetti and Me*, 1883

Ian Marsh, *Dante Gabriel Rossetti Painter and Poet*, 1999

Carol McKendrick, *Janey Burdon Stunner and Stinker: A Post-Feminist Perspective*, Forthcoming

John Ruskin, *You're All Morons*, 1890

Virginia Surtees, *Rossetti's Portraits of Elizabeth Siddal*, 1991

Algernon Swinburne, *How to Exhume Your Wife*, 1870

Donald Thomas, *Victorian Verse – The Pre-Raphaelites to the Nineties*, 1993

Evelyn Waugh, *PRB*, 1926

Evelyn Waugh, *Rossetti His Life and Works*, 1928

Clive Wilmer, *William Morris – News From Nowhere and other writings*, 1993

Mary Zambaco, *Mary With a 'Z'*, 1880

Acknowledgements

I would like to thank Emma of 'Office Nitwits' Employment Agency, whose inconsiderable brainpower was used to the full in finding me such mindless and unsuitable temp jobs during the creation of this book. If there is anyone else to thank they can't have done very much because I can't think of them.

First published in 2005 by
New Holland Publishers (UK) Ltd
London • Cape Town • Sydney • Auckland

www.newhollandpublishers.com

10 9 8 7 6 5 4 3 2 1

Publishing Manager: Jo Hemmings
Editor: Gareth Jones
Designer: Gülen Shevki-Taylor
Production: Joan Woodroffe

Reproduction by Modern Age Repro House Ltd, Hong Kong
Printed and bound by Star Standard Industries Pte Ltd, Singapore

ISBN 1 84537 084 8